KIERAN E. SCOTT

D ● T

PENGUIN BOOKS

this book is for you

Hello

how are you?

Are you OK?

Or

are you feeling

a little bit

or a lottle bit

anxious?

Well, if you are

I'm here to help.

Just look at me

and take your time.

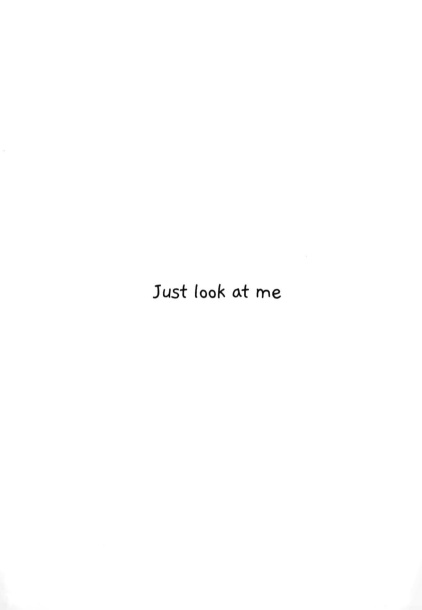

Just look at me

it will be fine.

My name is DOT.

So nice to meet you.

What do you think

a dot can do?

I can turn left

I can turn right.

I can look up

at the moon and the sun

or down at the ground

where your feet like to run.

If you breathe on me gently

I might change shape.

But before we begin

we need to prepare

so blow your breath out

get rid of that air.

Now take a deep breath

in through your nose

and blow your breath out

all the way from your toes.

Breathe in

and blow.

Breathe in

and blow.

Breathe in

and blow.

Breathe in

and blow.

That's really good breathing

it's so fun for me

to imagine with you

all the things

I can be.

Hey, guess what?

Did you know

that from very small things

big things can grow?

So breathe in again

and start to blow.

Breathe in

and blow.

Breathe in

and blow.

Breathe in

and blow.

Breathe in

and blow.

Wow! That was cool

you're breathing so well

you did a great job

I hope that it helped.

If you ever feel anxious

or a little stressed out

DOT will be here

I'm always about.

Dedicated to Elodie.

Kieran E. Scott is a New Zealand
photographer who accidentally
wrote a children's book.

PENGUIN

UK | USA | Canada | Ireland | Australia
India | New Zealand | South Africa | China

Penguin is an imprint of the Penguin Random House group of companies,
whose addresses can be found at global.penguinrandomhouse.com.

Penguin
Random House
New Zealand

First published by Penguin Random House New Zealand, 2020

1 3 5 7 9 10 8 6 4 2

© Kieran E. Scott, 2020

The moral right of the author has been asserted.

Book design by Katrina Duncan © Penguin Random House New Zealand
Printed and bound in China by RR Donnelley

A catalogue record for this book is available from
the National Library of New Zealand.

ISBN 978-0-14-377532-4

penguin.co.nz

MIX
Paper from
responsible sources
FSC® C144853